Dear Parent:
Your child's love of reading starts here!

Every child learns to read in a different way and at his or her own speed. Some go back and forth between reading levels and read favourite books again and again. Others read through each level in order. You can help your young reader improve and become more confident by encouraging his or her own interests and abilities. From books your child reads with you to the first books he or she reads alone, there are I Can Read Books for every stage of reading:

SHARED READING
Basic language, word repetition, and whimsical illustrations, ideal for sharing with your emergent reader

BEGINNING READING
Short sentences, familiar words, and simple concepts for children eager to read on their own

READING WITH HELP
Engaging stories, longer sentences, and language play for developing readers

READING ALONE
Complex plots, challenging vocabulary, and high-interest topics for the independent reader

ADVANCED READING
Short paragraphs, chapters, and exciting themes for the perfect bridge to chapter books

I Can Read Books have introduced children to the joy of reading since 1957. Featuring award-winning authors and illustrators and a fabulous cast of beloved characters, I Can Read Books set the standard for beginning readers.

A lifetime of discovery b⌐   ⌐ "I Can Read!"

Visit \
on enric

D0227724

DREAMWORKS®

SHREK THE THIRD™

Friends and Foes

First published in Great Britain in 2007 by HarperCollins Children's Books.
HarperCollins Children's Books is a division of HarperCollins Publishers Ltd.

1 3 5 7 9 10 8 6 4 2

ISBN-13: 978-0-00-724826-1
ISBN-10: 0-00-724826-1

Shrek the Third: Friends and Foes.

Printed and bound in Belgium

I Can Read!

READING
2
WITH HELP

DREAMWORKS

SHREK THE THIRD

Friends and Foes

Adapted by Catherine Hapka
Illustrations by Steven E. Gordon

HarperCollins Children's Books

Shrek is a big, green ogre.

He used to live alone in a swamp.

Then he married Fiona.

She talked him into
going to the big city.

Shrek doesn't like the city much.

He wants to go home to his swamp.

There is just one problem.

He might have to stay

and become king!

Fiona was once a beautiful princess.

A spell turned her into an ogre.

Fiona likes being an ogre princess.

Shrek likes her that way, too.

He likes that Fiona is strong and green.

Fiona knows that Shrek
doesn't want to be king.
He isn't very good at king stuff,
like making people knights.

Donkey is Shrek's best friend.

He goes everywhere with Shrek,

whether Shrek likes it or not.

He even goes with him

to find another king.

Donkey loves Dragon.

Their children are called dronkeys.

They all come to say good-bye

as Shrek and Donkey set sail.

Puss In Boots goes on the boat trip, too.

He is very brave.

Puss was once Shrek's foe.

But now they are good friends.

Puss is willing to fight
with sword, claws, and teeth.
But sometimes he just uses
his big, sad, cute eyes.

Shrek is looking for
Arthur Pendragon.
Arthur is called Artie for short.
Artie can become the next king
instead of Shrek.

There's just one problem.

Artie doesn't want the job.

It sounds like too much work.

Shrek gets Artie on the boat.

But Artie crashes it on the beach.

There they find a wizard named Merlin.

Merlin is a little strange.

But he can make magic.

He sends them back to the city

so Artie can become king.

Nasty Prince Charming

dreams of being king.

He even puts on plays about it!

There's just one problem.

He must get rid of Shrek

if he wants to rule the kingdom.

Prince Charming needs help
from some really bad guys.
He goes to an inn
where lots of villains hang out.

Captain Hook is a pirate.

Pirates are mean and greedy.

But Hook is crazy, too.

Cyclops has only half as many eyes
as most people.

But he's twice as mean.

Soon Charming has a whole evil army.
They help him take over the kingdom.
The Headless Horseman flies into town
on the back of a broomstick.

Charming has also gathered evil trees,

evil queens, evil dwarves,

and evil witches.

They head for the castle.

Shrek's fairy-tale friends
fight back against the bad guys.
Gingy is a smart cookie.
He helps the princesses get away.

The wolf and the three little pigs
help Pinocchio block the door.
There is just one problem:
Charming's army is very strong.

Charming throws Fiona in a cell
with Queen Lillian and the princesses.
The queen really uses her head.
She uses it to knock a hole in the wall.

"Mom?" Fiona says in surprise.

The queen smiles.

"Your fighting skills don't come from your father," says the queen.

28

Now the princesses are free

to help save the kingdom!

Snow White calls her forest friends

to fight the guards.

Cinderella uses her glass slipper

as a boomerang.

Even Sleeping Beauty helps.

She falls asleep and trips the guards.

The fairy-tale villains face off against the fairy-tale friends.

And Charming has captured Shrek.
But Artie arrives just in time
to save the day.

Artie will make a great king.

Shrek is off the hook.

Finally, he and Fiona can go home

to their Swamp Sweet Swamp.

Problem solved!